Remembering the 1940s

Remembering the 1940s

The Coats Family in Minnesota and Iowa

Deane Dierksen

Genealogy House
Amherst, Massachusetts

CHILDHOOD MEMORIES — some are real and some are what we were told later or what someone else remembered. Occasionally a "memory" is what we wish had happened. This paper is my effort to remember life in my family during the 1940s. In recent years I have asked my three siblings to comment on aspects of our family life. Our combined comments and memories (more my memories than theirs), family photos and documents, and additional research form the basis for this reminiscence.

In 1940 and 1941 my parents, Louis David "Bill" Coats (1910-1994) and Ouida Sturges (Moulton) Coats (1913-1982), lived briefly in Detroit Lakes, Minnesota, and Lidgerwood, North Dakota, before moving to St. Paul, Minnesota, in May 1941. Dad had worked in the poultry business for Swift and Company throughout the 1930s. Swift transferred its workers often and on short notice; Mom later remembered transfers with only twenty-four hours' notice. In 1939, when she was nearly nine months pregnant with my brother David, the company refused Dad's request to postpone a move until after the baby arrived. He moved and Mom went to Pierre, South Dakota, where her parents lived and where David was born October 1st. Mom later said Dad never forgave Swift. By August 1940 he was with the Ortonville Produce Company in Lidgerwood, North Dakota. One year later the family was in St. Paul where we lived in a duplex on Juliet Avenue. My brother Doug was born there on November 2, 1941.

Coats family: Ouida, Bill, Deane, David - Dec. 1940

Deane and David, 1941

WORLD WAR II

On 7 December 1941 I was five years old and in kindergarten. No doubt my parents, like the rest of the country, were glued to the radio, but I have no memory of that day. If they ever talked about Pearl Harbor day later I don't recall it. Years later Dad believed a conspiracy theory that President Roosevelt had met in a hotel room-somewhere with someone-and planned or agreed to the Pearl Harbor attack to take the country into the war.

Chicken pox is what I remember from that time. I brought it home from school and promptly passed it onto my little brothers, one after the other. David was just past two and Doug was five weeks old on December 7th. Mom later recalled that when Doug was only six weeks old he had chicken pox with a grand total of twenty-seven pox while David was nearly covered from head to toe with pox. In those days, before immunizations for childhood diseases like chicken pox, mumps, and measles had been developed, children with those diseases were quarantined. This meant a sign in the window warning people to stay away. Besides chicken pox, we had at least one other childhood disease that year and

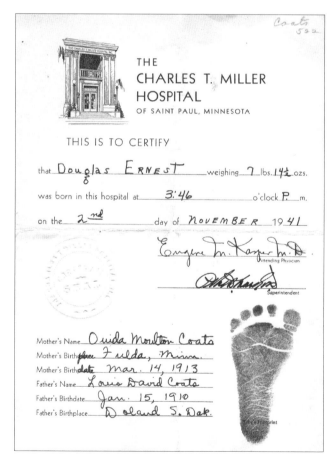
Douglas' birth certificate

were quarantined a lot. My great-uncle, Chester Sturges, a physician at the Minnesota Veterans Hospital, made the diagnosis and placed the signs in the window at the request of his niece, my mother.

By mid-year 1942 we had moved to Perry, Iowa, a town of about six thousand not far from Des Moines, where we lived until September 1949. My parents thought jobs would be frozen[1] as part of the war effort and wanted to be in a smaller town before that happened. Priebe and Sons, the poultry processing plant where Dad was the superintendent, was right beside tracks of the Milwaukee Road.[2] We often went to the plant after dinner so he could check on things. Frequently we kids watched crowded troop trains go by and waved at the troops. The plant was running several shifts, packing poultry for the army. Because of this Dad was classified as in an essential industry and was not drafted.

Doug, Deane, and David,
March 1942

Shortages on the home front were a fact of life. I remember Mom rolling her own rather lop-sided cigarettes with a little oblong machine. Women's stockings had a seam up the back in those days and were mostly unavailable. Mom, like many other women, sometimes used so-called "bottled stockings," a liquid leg make-up designed to look like stockings. The problem was that the "stockings" rubbed off on clothes and furniture. To mimic the seam, she drew a line up the back of her legs with an eyebrow pencil. She

Doug in stroller, partial
view of David, July 1942

---

1 April 17 1943, "The War Department Manpower Commission freezes essential workers in war industries, preventing some 27 million workers from leaving their jobs." Carl J. and Dorothy Schneider, *World War II* (New York: Facts On File, 2003), page 56, online in Google books, 8 November 2011.

2 Officially the Chicago, Milwaukee, St. Paul and Pacific Railroad (The Milwaukee Road). The Milwaukee Road Historical Association, www. mrha. com, viewed 8 November 2011

Doug, David, and Deane, 1943
— Deane's favorite photo

probably skipped the "stocking" much of the time and just went with the seam.

We had ration books and stamps for food, shoes, and clothing. We saved grease, fat, and tin foil and bought savings bonds in stamp books at school for the war effort. All three children had growing feet so gathering enough coupons for new shoes was a frequent concern. It also seemed we ate chicken all the time because it wasn't rationed. For many years afterward I disliked it.

Long after the war Mom told my sister Donna about the time she and Dad and another couple tried to get around rationing of red meat by rustling a cow. The details are vague, but some how they killed the cow and the men butchered it. But then they were afraid to use the meat for fear of being caught! David heard another version of the same incident, probably from Dad. In that version they bought the cow in Jamaica, Iowa, butchered it in a barn there, but again were afraid to use the meat for fear of being caught. What happened afterwards or what they did with the carcass remains a mystery.

The housing shortage caused our family major problems that did not end with the war. During our seven years in Perry we lived in six rented houses and very briefly in the one house we owned there. When the rental houses were sold, we had to move. Almost every move required a change of schools for us children. The sixth rental was a duplex at 708 First Street, across from the Perry Milk Products plant, where we lived for almost three years, from late spring 1946 to early January 1949.

New appliances and repair parts for old ones were unavailable during the war. In one of the early houses our refrigerator died and couldn't be replaced so we had to put an ice box on the back porch. Big blocks of ice were delivered periodically, but not often enough. The box always smelled stale-and wasn't cold enough to cool the milk well, much less keep ice cream.

New cars and parts for old ones were about as available as refrigerators. Dad and Mom drove what could best be called a rattle-trap. It was unreliable and getting gas for it was difficult. Long car trips were out of the question. When Mom took my brothers and me to visit her parents in Pierre, South Dakota, we went by train. I remember somehow getting gum in my hair on several trips and having to have it, with the chunk of hair caught in it, cut out with scissors. Trains were crowded then, with jump seats that folded down across the aisle. I don't remember how anyone passed along the aisle when the jump seats were in use. I do remember that the toilets were locked when the train was in a station because they emptied directly on to the tracks when flushed!

Small towns in the Midwest had air raids and black outs even though enemy air attacks were extremely unlikely. If a black out occurred on the night Bing Crosby's radio show was on Mom covered the radio with an overcoat to prevent the light from radio tubes from showing through the window. She did not want to miss her favorite show.

To support the war effort, our family, like many others, planted a vegetable garden and canned fruits and vegetables at home. For at least one season we had a fairly large victory garden. We had to drive to it because it was at the edge of town. No one in the family liked working in the garden but we did it, usually in the evening after dinner. I think one season is all we managed! Mom did lots of canning, during and after the war. Early on she used sterilized glass canning jars. Later she borrowed a canning machine that used metal cans and sealed them. My memory of this activity mostly covers the post war period when she canned tomatoes, peas, green beans, and peaches. We had so many home canned peaches, which many people considered special,

Doug, Deane, and David, 1944 — Ouida's favorite photo

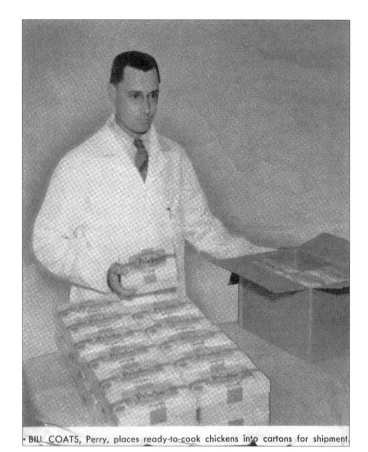

Front page of The Chanticleer, *September 1946, published for friends and employees of PRIEBE & SONS, Inc.*

that I grew to hate them. All during the Perry years she also made jelly. After cooking the jelly, she put it in glass jars and poured wax over the top to seal the contents before putting on a lid. We had to be careful when removing the wax to prevent pieces from ending up in the jelly.

Three of Dad's six brothers served in the army, one in Europe, two in the Pacific. I remember Mom baking fruit cakes to send to the brothers. She disliked fruit cake but she made it because fruit cakes would keep for long periods and mail delivery to battle areas was uncertain. Fortunately all three brothers survived the war and lived to old age.

Local theaters played newsreel and feature films about World War II. I have never forgotten the 1944 movie about the five Sullivan brothers. They served together in the navy and all five went down on the same ship in 1942. The scene I remember is when the family got the news that all the boys were gone. As the result of this tragedy, the military changed its policy so that all the sons of one family could not serve together and a sole surviving son was released from the draft or combat duty.

A children's book about the war that impressed me was *Snow Treasure* by Marie McSwigan. Suggested by a true story, it is about Norwegian children who helped save their country's gold reserves from the Nazis by sledding out with gold bricks fastened under their sleds. It never occurred to me then or later to wonder if this were really possible. I must have read the book soon after it came out in 1943. By the time I came to work at the Falls Church library, I remembered the story but not the title. It was like finding an old friend when I ran across it in the 1970s.

"You're a Sap Mr. Jap, Don't You Know the Yankee Spanky" was an often-heard popular song; I think we had a recording of it. Another song I remember was "Praise the Lord and Pass the Ammunition."

Finally the war was over and everyone celebrated. A local history described the scene in Perry: "With shouts, laughter, showers of shredded paper and wild honking of auto horns, Perry residents celebrated the end of World War II all through the night and into the early hours of Wednesday August 14 and 15, 1945. The impromptu ceremony started spontaneously shortly after the news came at 6 p.m. Tuesday and gained momentum as it went along."[3]

My clear memory is of one person who was not honking her horn-my mother. Mom was just as glad as anyone about the end of the war, but she didn't believe in driving around honking her horn. I still remember how disappointed I was over that!

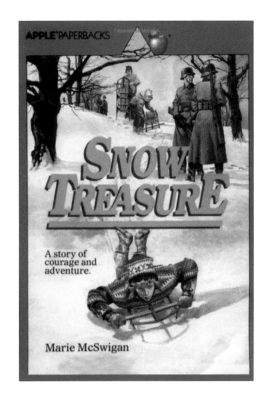

3   Marjorie Patterson, *History of Perry, Iowa* (12 volume typescript, FHL # 1580055, the author, ca 1988) VIII, pp. 51- 52.

Webster Elementary School. Built in 1913 and 1914 on the east side of Third Street between North and Paul Streets, Webster Elementary School opened on March 9, 1914. Originally named the Third or North Ward School, its new name was chosen in hopes that "children would be as bright as Noah or Daniel Webster." It closed with the new Perry Elementary School opened in the fall of 1992 and has since been demolished.

Pamela J. Jenkins and Martha A. Tanner. Perry (Charleston, SC: Arcadia Publishing, 2008) 74.

Perry had three elementary (K-6) schools then: Webster, Roosevelt, and Lincoln. Almost every move put us in a different school district, so we attended each school, some of them several times. In kindergarten or first grade our teacher asked the students put their heads down on their desks to rest. She always commended the child who could be the most still during this period. I tried and tried to be completely still but never succeeded. Of course some children went straight to sleep but I never did.

I skipped second grade, thanks to Mom's triumph over Superintendent J. S. Vanderlinden. I had attended kindergarten in St. Paul where reading was not part of that year's curriculum. It was taught in Perry's kindergarten. The superintendent didn't think anyone who hadn't had that experience could succeed in their first grade. Mom asked him to let me try it. But Vanderlinden was not willing to give me a chance. Instead he said if I started first grade then, he would have me flunked back into kindergarten after the first six weeks — their policy with first graders who didn't measure up! Mom was not willing to risk that, so I repeated kindergarten. But she didn't give up on getting me where she thought I belonged. They finally agreed that I could be tutored during the summer after first grade and enter third grade that fall. All I remember about being tutored is walking to the tutor's house. Educationally skipping a grade worked out well. Socially it worked less well. Some children in both the new and old grades thought the move was unfair and resented me for it.

David and Doug, with October 1st and November 2nd birthdays, each had to wait a year to start school because the school birthday deadline was September 30th. The only option was the Catholic school. My Protestant parents would not consider this, a decision that Mom later somewhat regretted. She felt David was ready for school and that his education had suffered for having been delayed a year. She did not feel it hurt Doug as much.

We went to Roosevelt School when we lived at 708 First Street. In my memory and Doug's, it was a long walk-Doug remembers twelve blocks and that seems right. At least some of the time we walked home for lunch during our one-hour lunch period. The teacher I most remember is Miss Cecilia Covey, a *very* heavy older woman who taught geography and probably didn't bathe as often as she might have. She liked to walk around and then perch on the corner of a student 's desk during class. No one wanted her to sit on their desk! Another teacher I remember is Miss Williams, the grade-school music teacher. From her I learned many things, including that the Lone Ranger music was from *The William Tell Overture*!

Girl Scouts Of Troop No. 6 1948
Perry, Iowa

Girl Scouts of Troop No. 6 are pictured following their meeting Wednesday evening at the Bills Tea Room.

Back row, from left, Nancy Edwards, JoAnne Payton, Hil- degarde Liebe, Claudette Thompson, and Shirley Randall.

-Front row from left, Janet Fiscel, Elsie Christensen, Marie Phillips, Shirley Bruce, JoAnn Crannell, Elaine Becker and Deane Coats. Norma Jean Riley was not present.

Mrs. Wayne Swift is the leader of troop No. 6 and Mrs. Marlowe Becker is assistant leader.

During our grade-school years Mom made candy-fudge, caramels, divinity,[4] and rolled cookies with a date filling for our teachers at Christmas. Miss Hardy, who taught David and Doug in first grade, supposedly said she was glad to get another Coats child in her class so she would get the Christmas candy. At any rate, we all believed we had something special to give our teachers. We all still remember that candy, especially those caramels.

School life in the 1940s differed in many ways from today. No elementary school I attended had clubs or extra-curricular activities. We never had home work, not even once that I recall. We didn't have team sports in elementary school except occasionally in physical education. I don't remember ever taking a field trip. Scout troops were independent from the schools. By about the fourth grade I joined a Girl Scout troop led by Mrs. Swift. My only memory of the troop is of her husband playing the musical saw for us.

---

4   Divinity is a white candy, the principal ingredients of which are sugar, light corn syrup, egg whites, and nuts.

FAMILY LIFE AND ACTIVITY, 1942 – 1949

We did not live near any relatives after leaving Minnesota. Travel was not as easy then as now and money was always tight so we never spent holidays with relatives. Holiday and birthday parties and celebrations didn't seem so important then. Apparently that was not just in our family. In her memoir of growing up in Iowa at a slightly later date, Susan Allen Toth said, "When I was growing up, Ames did not pay much attention to most holidays."[5] Ames is about forty miles from Perry.

Ouida fourth from the right, front row.

We kept in touch with relatives and friends far away by writing letters. For local communication we had a telephone, just one, and it had a dial. Part of the time in Perry, you placed a call by picking up the receiver and telling the operator at Central what number you wanted. A song I heard a number of times is titled, "Hello, Central, Give Me Heaven for My Mommy's There." Long distance telephone calls were largely reserved for emergencies. If you got a long distance call it was usually bad news—somebody was dead or dying or had suffered some kind of disaster.

I have only a few Christmas memories. We always opened gifts on Christmas Eve and Santa did not wrap the gifts he brought to the Coats children. Mom said he had too many homes to visit to have time to wrap all the presents. After Christmas Eve dinner, while Mom did the dishes, Dad took us children for a ride around town to look at Christmas decorations. It never failed that Santa came while we were out. As far as I know none of us ever caught on while we still believed in Santa Claus. I have only one memory of a childhood Christmas gift. In 1946, when I was in fifth grade, David and I both got bicycles, our first. Doug got some kind of vehicular toy, perhaps a pedal airplane. This was the first year after the war that metal was available for children's toys.

---

5 Susan Allen Toth, *Blooming: A Small-Town Girlhood* (Boston: Little, Brown, 1981), 81.

In Perry, Mom belonged to two bridge clubs; one played auction bridge, the other contract bridge. She was also active in the Eastern Star,[6] sang in the Presbyterian Church choir and was active in the women's organization of the church. Dad belonged to the Masons and the Elks or B. P. O. E. for Benevolent Protective Order of Elks. He told us it meant Best People on Earth. When they went out as a couple we had teen-age baby sitters. One of our sitters was crazy about Frank Sinatra, who was all the rage then. Teen-age girls swooned over him and made a big production of it. Mom was afraid the sitter wouldn't pay attention to us if Frank Sinatra was on the radio!

Priebe plant, Perry, Iowa, 1948

Dad also participated in athletic activities whenever he could. In the summer our noon meal, which we called dinner, was our main meal so he could play golf after work. He also played on weekends. In the winter he bowled and one summer he coached a local men's softball team. I remember attending some of those games at the ball field in the city park.

In the 1940s my family ate a bit differently than most of us do today. Our basic evening meal—supper—was meat and potatoes. Beef was the meat of choice, though rationing affected this during the war. We also ate pork chops, ham, and chicken, much more of the latter than I liked. Peas, green beans, carrots, corn, and tomatoes were our vegetables. If fresh vegetables were not available, we ate canned vegetables. We had asparagus (canned) from time to time because Dad liked it; he taught us children to eat it as well as green olives, another of his favorites. My favorite meal was pork chops, mashed potatoes, and peas. David remembers that Mom made good scalloped potatoes and ham.

Many foods that are common today did not appear on our table. I never heard of broccoli until I was much older and don't remember ever being served cauliflower. We didn't eat rice. If we didn't have potatoes as a starch we had macaroni or spaghetti-we

6 "The Order of the Eastern Star is a fraternal organization that both men and women can join. It was established in 1850 by Rob Morris, ... who had been an official with the Freemasons. It is based on teachings from the Bible, but is open to people of all theistic beliefs. It has approximately 10,000 chapters in twenty countries and approximately 500,000 members under its General Grand Chapter. Members of the Order are aged 18 and older; men must be Master Masons and women must have specific relationships with Masons. Originally, a woman would have to be the daughter, widow, wife, sister, or mother of a master Mason, but the Order now allows other relatives as well as allowing Job's Daughters, Rainbow Girls, Members of the Organization of Triangle (NY only) and members of the Constellation of Junior Stars (NY only) to become members when they become of age." Wikipedia, "The Order of the Eastern Star, " viewed 9 November 2011.

never used the word pasta. Mom cooked only foods she thought we would eat, so our diet was not terribly varied. Once in a while Dad brought home oysters and made oyster stew; none of us children liked it. I wouldn't even eat the stew without the oysters. If one of us children did not like what was served, our choices were a bowl of cereal or go hungry. We did not have an open kitchen!

My brother Doug thinks Mom was a terrible cook. She certainly was not a great cook, but she cooked in the style of the day in the Midwest. This included over-cooked beef. I think she cooked because that was her job, not because she loved to cook. But she shone when she prepared desserts and sweets[7]: candy, pies, cookies. Her apple pie was outstanding, one of the few desserts that Dad cared to eat. He and Mom liked it with a slice of Velveeta, their all-purpose cheese of choice, on it.

We had several varieties of cookies on a regular basis—raisin oatmeal, Wheaties coconut, and peanut butter. One easy and tasty dessert consisted of layers of graham cracker squares, crushed canned pineapple with juice, and whipped cream, in that order. We loved it. Another favorite was Mom's chocolate sauce. She made it without measuring the ingredients. She put cocoa, sugar, milk, and maybe butter in a sauce pan and cooked it over high heat till it looked right to her. If we were lucky it would freeze hard on ice cream. We loved that, too.

Popcorn was a big favorite in our family. We all loved the red popcorn stand on a main corner down town. A farm woman in a white uniform ran it. It was open only on Saturdays, when all the farmers came to town. I remember it as the world's best popcorn. The popcorn lady said that for good grub, you had to salt it at the proper time in the cooking cycle. I can't remember now whether the proper time was before or after cooking. David remembers that she made white popcorn and sold it in bags up to grocery bag size. On special occasions she also sold a bag of "old maids"—the kernels that don't pop—for very little.

Dad often made popcorn at home. He used a deep cast aluminum pan that was warped on the bottom from over heating and black around the sides from frequent use. He put oil in the pan and heated it until it sizzled from a drop of water, added white Jolly Time popcorn, put the lid on, and shook the pan over the burner until the corn popped. Afterward he

---

7   See recipes for caramels and several of the cookies at the end of this paper.

melted butter in the pan and poured it over the popped corn. This long-gone pan became a family icon because it is the same pan Mom used to make her famous caramels.

Going to Moxley's Ice Cream Parlor was a special treat. My favorite flavor was butter brickle, one I did not see for many years after we left Perry. I only remember going to Moxley's when Dad took us. Soda, or pop as it was called in Perry, was a rare treat. Once or twice a year Dad would bring home a six-pack of Grapette and it was gone almost before he could set the carton down. Very occasionally Mom treated us to a cherry Coke at the drug store soda fountain. And about once a year she made Hershey sandwiches, something she remembered having at a local drug store during her school days. They were grilled with a Hershey bar in the middle instead of cheese and would not make anybody's nutritionally correct list today!

Radio was *the* medium of entertainment and news in the 1940s. It loomed large in our lives. Early in our time in Perry we had a floor-model radio. Later we had a table-model Philco radio record player that we children were allowed to operate. To play a record, we opened the door, slid the record in, shut the door, and it played automatically. We had Glenn Miller and Freddie Slack records, but the ones I most remember were old Victor one-sided opera recordings, with the logo of a dog listening to "His Master's Voice." Mom got them from her mother. I listened to many of them over and over. To this day I recognize the sextet from the opera "Lucia di Lamermoor" by the first three notes. The singers on that one included Enrico Caruso and Ezio Pinza.

In the morning Mom listened to the Breakfast Club with Don McNeill. It was a forerunner of morning variety type shows and was on for many years. I particularly remember that McNeill played a march every morning and I marched around the kitchen to it. Both parents, but especially Mom, listened to all the mystery shows on in the evening: Mr. Keen, Tracer of Lost Persons; The Shadow ("who knows what evil lurks in the hearts of man... the Shadow knows"); "Mr. District Attorney"; and others. They also listened to comedy shows with Jack Benny and others. Dad liked listening to sports broadcasts. Mom liked the musical shows such as The Telephone Hour, The Railroad Hour, and the Voice of Firestone, all featuring classical and semi-classical music. I liked those, too, especially the operettas on the Railroad Hour in which Gordon Mac Rae played and sang most of the male leads.

David hated Monday night radio because the Voice of Firestone was on and conflicted with something he wanted to hear. We had only one radio.

Dad was a tremendous fan of "The Lone Ranger" and it wasn't advisable to interrupt while it was on. It was a staple of my childhood, airing three nights a week at 6:30 p.m. Brace Beemer played the lead role—he had a distinctive voice. The Lone Ranger "was a knight of the range, a western hero who quickly became part of popular American folklore." He spoke perfect English, didn't smoke, drink, or swear, and was in all ways an exemplary hero. One writer said "If a cynic should doubt that all this purity could possibly be accepted by a large listening public for more than 20 years, he should perhaps be excused as a product of a different and less noble time."[8] Hi-Yo Silver!

Radio stations broadcast many programs for children. I remember sitting on the floor on Sundays with the comic section from the Sunday paper in front of me while I listened to uncle somebody read the funnies. Des Moines had an uncle show in the 1940s that featured or copied the most famous uncle, "Uncle Don," who was on for over twenty years. His daily show included songs, stories, jokes, birthday mentions, and advice.[9] On weekday afternoons children's adventure programs came on. Some favorites were Jack Armstrong, All-American Boy; Sky King; and Sergeant Preston of the Northwest Mounted Police and his dog King. Many were sponsored by cereal manufacturers and offered premiums such as a special decoder ring for a certain number of box tops. Mom made us eat all the cereal in a box before she let us have the box top.

When I was in seventh grade and home sick for a few days I got hooked on radio soap operas or "pain-per-minute dramas."[10] A number of such programs played in the afternoon. For a while after that I hated to go to school because I had to miss installments of my favorites!

Princess Elizabeth of England, now Queen Elizabeth II, was much in the media of the day—radio and newspapers. When she married Prince Philip 20 November 1947, newspapers printed full information on the wedding. I sat in front of the radio during the

---

8 John Dunning, *On the Air: The Encyclopedia of Old Time* Radio (New York: Oxford University Press, 1998), 405.

9 Dunning, *On the Air*, 688.

10 Dunning , *On the Air*, 635.

live broadcast of the ceremony with the newspaper diagram in front of me, following every detail. She fascinated me because we share a birthday, her real birthday in April, not the public one she celebrates in June. I still follow news about her.

Perry's public library was a big old Carnegie building with what seemed then like a long flight of stairs up to the front door, probably standard Carnegie architecture. Mom was a frequent library patron in Perry as everywhere we lived. She took me to the children's room when I was about in third grade and showed me a shelf with a series of animal stories that I just loved. I can still see that shelf. Probably Thornton Burgess or Ernest Thompson Seton wrote those stories. I also liked comic books and Nancy Drew books but they were not available at the library. At that time librarians disapproved of both—not high enough quality!

There were fewer organized activities for children then. In our early years in Perry, my favorite play activity was playing cowboys and Indians with other children in the neighborhood. I had a play gun and holster so I could be a cowboy. Mostly what we did was run around chasing each other. Later in the decade I loved to roller skate on the sidewalk. The skates fit onto regular shoes—I always had hard-soled shoes—with clamps on the side that were fitted with a key I wore on a chain around my neck when skating.

Piano and dancing lessons were available. I took dancing lessons for six years starting when I was about six or seven, mostly I think because my mother always wanted to take dancing and didn't get to. We had a teacher named Bette Mae Harris, with bleached blonde hair, who had been a professional dancer some place. People didn't have tape or CD players then, so Bette Mae hired a woman we called Auntie Faye (Mullen) to play the piano accompaniment. At lessons she smoked cigarettes all day, very often had a glass beer beside her and played one-handed when she took a sip. At practice she played the music strictly up to tempo and we were supposed to keep up with her. At recitals, she played whatever speed we danced! I was not a great dancer, to say the least.

Carnegie Library. The town's library, built with a $10,000 grant from Andrew Carnegie, opened in 1904 with 1,000 titles donated by the Perry community. Its first librarian was Flora Bailey, who served in the position until 1945. The Perry Public Library had its home in the building until 1994, when it moved to a new building across the street. In 2004, the building had a grand reopening as the Carnegie Library Museum, part of Hometown Perry, Iowa.

Pamela J. Jenkins and Martha A. Tanner. Perry. (Charleston, SC: Arcadia Publishing, 2008) 93.

My parents acquired a piano during our last year in Perry. Dad somehow got it from someone who had stored it in an unused farm building, maybe a chicken coop. It was not pretty and required a lot of clean-up, but according to the piano tuner the sounding board was good. I started lessons then and continued them into high school. I used the John Thompson red piano books that were the standard at the time. I enjoyed piano lessons more than dancing and was a better pianist than dancer. Faint praise!

We had a lot of magazines in our house. I loved the children's magazines we subscribed to, especially *Children's Playmate* and *Jack and Jill*. They often had

Dance recital, June 1949. The "Juniorettes on Toe." Deane at far left in front row.

continued stories and I would save the issues to read the whole story at one time. Mom subscribed to mystery magazines, *The Saturday Evening Post*, and many of the women's magazines. She did not like *Good Housekeeping* or *Life* but I never knew why. When new issues arrived, only essential chores got done until Mom had read the mall.

We played many card and board games. "Sorry" was one, about which more below. Occasionally Dad played checkers with us; he never lost a game on purpose. If we ever won, it was not a gift. Monopoly was a big favorite with me. A friend and I played games that continued for weeks or months—this was about fourth or fifth grade. It was possible to end up winning or losing great amounts of play money. Sometimes we even ran out of Monopoly money!

I played two card games with my brothers when they were small: War and Go Fish. War especially could get rather raucous when we were slapping down cards to take a trick. Mom taught me several ways to play solitaire. Also we had a card game called "Authors" which had its own deck of cards with faces of famous authors; the list of authors changed over time. I remember Robert Louis Stevenson, William Makepeace Thackeray, Alfred Lord Tennyson, and Louisa May Alcott. The goal was to match the authors with their books. Each author had four books listed. I learned about a lot of famous books that way though I can't say I have read them all even yet!

Another memory of Perry is going to the movies. The town had two theaters, the Perry and the Dallas, both on the same block; the movies changed every week. One theater showed so-called A movies, the big name ones, and I went there often on Sundays. The other theater showed B movies, mostly cowboy movies, and it always had an adventure serial with cliff-hanger endings each week; I went there on Saturdays. My favorite cowboy movies were those with Gene Autry and the ones about the Durango Kid, played by Charles Starrett. The A movie theater had lots of musicals and family features such as stories featuring Lassie or other animals. Margaret O'Brien was a famous child star then and I loved her movies. Admission for a child was ten cents. My twenty-five cent allowance got me in to both movies. On Sunday I could spend the extra nickel for something from the snack bar. I liked popcorn but probably bought Milk Duds more often.

In the house we lived in the last year of the war, the Meldrums, a childless couple whom we called Bobbie and Mrs. Meldrum, were our back door neighbors. The Meldrums were nice to all of us but thought the sun rose and set in David; Doug also remembers feeling special. They seemed ancient to me at the time, but Bobbie was still working on the railroad as an engineer or fireman. They introduced our family to Sorry, a board game in which each player tries to move his pieces around the board faster than the other players. When one player knocks another player's piece back to Start, he says an insincere "Sorry! " That game is still around and I have played it with my children and grandchildren.

I had the measles in the house near the Meldrums. It was the two-week variety that can affect the eyes. Because of an eye problem I had to stay in bed in a darkened room for the whole two weeks. It seemed like forever.

It was also at this house that David had an unfortunate encounter with a dog and had to be rushed to the doctor for many stitches to his face and head. Doug's memory is that David got between a bitch in heat and a male dog trying to get to her. I remember coming home to an empty house, finding bloody towels all over, and not knowing what was going on. The dog was quarantined to see if it had rabies, but Mom thought it should be killed. I don't know what happened after the quarantine period, but the dog didn't have rabies. Fortunately David recovered from his injuries except for a few scars.

During one period in early spring 1946, no rental house was available in Perry. Mom and we children spent six or eight weeks with her parents in Pierre, South Dakota. This must have been difficult. Grandmother Bess Moulton was feeling the pressure after only two days!

> This is a very busy household! Ouida & 3 children arrived on the bus-Monday afternoon [11 March 1946] to stay until Bill can either beg, borrow or steal a place for them to live in. They hunted for a month in Perry & couldn't find anything even within a radius of 10 or 12 miles so Bill has a temporary room at a friends and Ouida & family are here. Deane & David started school—Tues A. M.—so it isn't too noisy part of the time but this is such a little house for so many people that our nerves are all on edge by night. However am glad we can give them a roof over their heads at least.[11]

After Pierre, we moved to 708 First Street where we lived for almost three years. It was a duplex and smaller than the earlier houses. We lived on the first floor, which had the front and back doors and only two bedrooms. Like our other houses, it had one bathroom with a tub but no shower. The upstairs unit had an outside stairway to the second floor; a variety of tenants lived there, none of whom I remember. An alley ran behind the house-in fact there may have been an alley behind all the houses in Perry. Occasionally tramps knocked on the back door and Mom fed them in exchange for chores. I think she was sympathetic

---

11 Letter from Bessie Sturges Moulton (913 E. Capitol Ave., Pierre, SD) to R. J. Moulton, Jr., and family, 13 March 1946; held by the author.

to their plight and looked for things for them to do so she could give them a meal.

We had a wringer washing machine in the basement. All wash loads used the same wash water and the same rinse water. After washing, Mom ran the clothes through a wringer. To rinse, she swung the wringer arm over to the other tubs. She started with whites and moved on down to darks; heavy items last. One time (here or in an earlier house) David somehow got his hand caught in the wringer. When Mom hit the release bar a piece flew off, hit him in the head, and he had to have stitches.

Ouida in front of 708 First Street, Perry, Iowa, 1947

Because there were no automatic clothes dryers at that time, Mom hung clothes out to dry on a clothes line in the back yard. If it was cold enough, the clothes froze until they were stiff as a board. After drying came ironing. Before fabric softeners almost everything needed ironing, a chore that Mom hated. To avoid ironing Dad's washable work pants, she struggled with metal pants stretchers, an adjustable device that she put into the wet pant legs. Then she expanded the stretchers as far as possible. If she placed them right, the legs dried with a perfect crease and she only had to iron around the top. They were a lot of work but she thought they were worth it.

I remember being sent regularly to the public swimming pool during the summer when I was ten or so. It was beyond the milk plant and I had to ride my bike through the city park to get there. The pool was small and crowded-I remember it being so crowded I literally couldn't move. I disliked going because the ride home left me hot and sticky. I also hated having to check my glasses-the lenses were actually glass, not plastic, then. We put our clothes in a wire basket, turned it in at the desk, and got a key that fastened to our suits. We stepped into a foot bath of disinfectant as we came out of the dressing room to go to the pool. At this time the pool was drained every week, starting after closing time on Sunday. The lifeguards spent Monday cleaning the pool; when it re-opened on Tuesday it had fresh water. The water was chlorinated, but obviously

Bill and David, with Perry Milk Products in background.

methods of keeping the water clean did not compare to today's filtration systems. Probably the cost of water was lower also.

Mostly we were all healthy during the Perry years. We were among the few children who didn't have routine tonsillectomies. I remember feeling deprived because I didn't get to stay home and have ice cream like other children did. But Mom could see no reason for it when we were healthy. Several polio scares occurred when we lived in Perry. This was before the development of polio vaccine. We knew a girl who got bulbar polio and was in an iron lung for a while. Fortunately she recovered completely. But it was a scary time—swimming pools were closed, and people were advised to keep children away from crowds. I also remember a *big* scandal about a local general practitioner, Dr. Elvidge, who lost his medical license for performing abortions. He may have been our doctor. At any rate Mom had some sympathy for him.

1705 Evelyn Street, Perry, Iowa, September 1949

1705 Evelyn Street, Perry, Iowa, September 1949

In January 1949 we moved into a new house on Evelyn Street, the first house our parents owned. This one-story house was small, with only two bedrooms, living dining room combination, kitchen, bathroom, and a full basement. It had a one-car garage and a dirt or gravel driveway. In old photos it looks like a cardboard house or a false front.

Mom did not want to buy this house because she thought it was too small. Dad was determined to buy it and agreed to build a bedroom for the boys in the basement. He and a friend did the work themselves. They finished the room in knotty pine and put war surplus bunk beds in it. Doug remembers these bunk beds earlier at 708 First Street and David falling out of the top bunk. I got the second bedroom on the main floor, a real treat for me because all three of us shared a bedroom at 708 First. The house did not have a separate dining room, only a dining area off the living room. We ate there because the kitchen was also small.

We lived in this house only until September. By then Dad had decided to leave Priebe & Sons and had taken a position as superintendent of a poultry processing plant in Estherville,

Iowa. Mom was pregnant, near term, and determined to move before the baby was born. She said it was easier to move with the baby in the tummy. We left Perry just in time. Our sister, Donna, was born on September 30th, about one week after the move, thereby beating the school enrollment birthday deadline by one day!

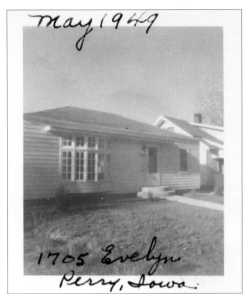

OUIDA'S RECIPES

CARAMELS

We do not know where Mom got this recipe. Her copy listed the ingredients but not the directions. We describe what Donna and I remember about how she did it. She always used the heavy pan mentioned above.

Brown   1 cup white sugar [use heavy pan!]

Add   1 cup thick cream and cook till smooth.

Add   2 cups sugar
           1 cup cream
           6 tablespoons butter.

[After these ingredients are added, cook slowly—this from Donna's and my experience.]

Cook to soft ball stage. Mom measured this by dropping a dollop of the batter into a cup of cool water. If it formed in to a soft ball, it was ready. If not, she cooked it some more, then checked again.

Each time she checked, she started with a clean cup and clean water. (My candy thermometer says soft ball stage is 240 degrees. Donna's note says she tried 248 degrees and it was probably too high.) Cool. Mom would put ice cubes and water in the sink and set the pan in it for a few minutes. She did not use a thermometer

Beat the heck out of it (till creamy). Mom would put a towel in her lap, set the pan on it, and beat by hand with a large spoon. She could tell by how it looked when it was "done."

Add nuts and vanilla. Mom gave no amounts but probably it should be 1 teaspoon vanilla and 1 cup nuts. Put in 8 or 9 inch square pan[not sure of pan size—perhaps larger] and refrigerate till set.

This recipe takes some skill to get right. When over cooked, it sugars—has a grainy texture—and doesn't taste as good. When under cooked, it still tastes just as good but never completely sets, and probably needs to beaten with a spoon. *Ancestry Magazine* published this as a Heritage Recipe in its November/December 2008 issue, page 17.

Donna commented on Mom's recipes in an email to me on 25 April 2008 :

"Most of Mother's recipes didn't include directions. As I recall, she always said that most cookies and cakes used what she called the butter/cream method. You beat the shortening or butter together with the sugar until it was well mixed. Then you added the eggs and beat well. Finally, you added the dry ingredients and mixed well. Mother never bothered with sifting; she thought it was a waste of time. Mostly, she made cookies with shortening as it was less expensive than using butter. When butter is used in the same recipes, there has to be some sort of adjustment to amounts (I'm not sure about the calculation for the adjustment) or the cookies will spread. I also recall that she didn't measure the shortening. She had a spoon that was perhaps slightly larger than a soup spoon. She would make a heaping scoop with the spoon. 3 scoops was a half cup and 6 scoops was a cup. I got used to that calculation and didn't measure the shortening either. I think she hated cleaning the measuring cup.

"I loved her oatmeal raisin cookies. The raisins were always plump—no doubt from being boiled and the cookies were small and high instead of being round and flat. . . . The soda cracker dessert is served with whipped cream (real whipped cream). She served it when she had bridge parties or similar events. She always said that no one believed the ingredients and I certainly thought it was remarkable. I have a hunch that this was a depression era/ wartime recipe when people had to get creative with ingredients because they didn't have much money."

RAISIN OATMEAL COOKIES

1 cup shortening	1 cup raisins	1 teaspoon cinnamon
2 eggs	1 cup sugar	1 teaspoon baking soda
2 cups oatmeal	1 teaspoon salt	
2 cups flour	1 teaspoon nutmeg	

Boil the raisins in water to cover for several minutes till raisins are plump. Add the baking soda. Cool slightly. [Use general directions above.] Cook 8-10 minutes at 375 degrees.

WHEATIES COCONUT COOKIES

1 cup shortening	2 cups coconut	½ teaspoon salt
1 cup brown sugar	2 ¼ cups flour	½ teaspoon vanilla
1 cup white sugar	2 cups Wheaties	1 teaspoon baking powder
2 eggs	1 teaspoon baking soda	

Follow Mom's general directions. The batter may have to be mixed with hands. After mixing, roll into balls. Put on greased cookie sheet and mash. (The sanitary way to mash is with a fork but I think we often bent our fingers and mashed with the lower part of our fingers.) Bake at 350 degrees for 9 minutes. Makes about 6 dozen.

SODA CRACKER DESSERT

Crumble 15 soda crackers	½ teaspoon baking powder
1 cup sugar	1 teaspoon vanilla
1 cup chopped nuts	

Mix well and fold into 2 egg whites that have been beaten until stiff. Turn out into cake or pie tin. Bake at 325 degrees for 20-25 minutes. Top with whipped cream (use heavy whipping cream). (Whipped cream substitutes such as Cool Whip were not yet available.)

Ouida

CPSIA information can be obtained at www.ICGtesting.com
Printed in the USA
BVIW120048081220
595085BV00009B/38